CLOSER THAN I THOUGHT

Thirty Lessons I Learned in My Thirties

KEVIN HORTON

Published independently.

First Edition

ISBN: 979-8-9951044-4-5

Cover design & Interior formatting: Mehrab Meraj

Printed in the United States of America

To the people who helped shape my thirty-year-old self

and the people who helped build the man I became at forty-two.

Your influence is written on every page.

Contents

Introduction

I remember sitting on the porch of my parents' house that weekend, looking out at the yard where I had spent so much of my childhood. Everything around me felt familiar, but life didn't feel familiar anymore. I was about to turn thirty, and instead of feeling accomplished, I felt uncertain. Like I had somehow missed a turn and didn't know how to get back on the road I was supposed to be on.

Mom, Dad, and my brother were home that weekend. It was Saturday morning, just a couple of days before my birthday. We had lived in that house since I was about fifteen years old, which meant we had been there longer than anywhere else I had lived growing up.

There was a swing in the yard where I had done a lot of thinking through the years. I had always loved that spot. I had sat there countless times growing up, thinking about the future.

I had come home because my family was planning a birthday party for me. It should have been a happy time, but I remember feeling something very different. I was thinking about where I was in life and wondering if I had actually accomplished anything at all.

Turning thirty felt heavier than any birthday before it.

My job was grinding on me. I didn't have a girlfriend. I didn't have children. I felt like I needed to be making more money. When I looked around at where other people seemed to be in life, I couldn't shake the feeling that I had fallen behind.

Looking back now, I realize a lot of that pressure came from focusing on the wrong things. I was too busy measuring my progress against other people's lives instead of running my own race. Competition has always brought out the best in me, but at that stage of life it had me focused in the wrong direction.

When I imagined what thirty was supposed to look like, I pictured a wife, maybe a couple of kids, a house, and a sense that things were settled. At the time, that seemed like the least likely outcome for me.

Ironically, within a year I would start dating the woman who would become my wife.

I was singing the blues, basically.

I wasn't hopeless, but I was stuck in that place where you feel like you're in limbo — not quite where you want to be, and not sure exactly how you're going to get there.

At some point that weekend I picked up my phone, an iPhone 5, opened the Notes app, and started writing.

I began listing things that felt true about life as I was approaching thirty. Observations about time, friendships, work, relationships, money, faith, and the way life seemed to change as you moved out of your twenties.

Once I started writing, the dam broke. One thought led to another until the list began to take shape.

I liked the symmetry of it — thirty thoughts as I was turning thirty.

Some were things I believed were already true. Some were things I aspired to. Some were things I thought I needed to start working toward.

By the time I finished, I had written thirty of them.

I didn't write the list for anyone else. I didn't think anyone would ever see it. It was simply a snapshot of what was going through my head at that moment in time.

Over the years, I've come back to that note every now and then.

Sometimes it's just out of curiosity. Sometimes it's a reminder to take stock of how far life has come since that moment.

What surprises me now when I read it is how unsure I sounded. At the time, work had me wondering whether I even belonged in the role I was in. Things that had once come naturally suddenly felt difficult.

Life eventually turned that around as well.

What I've realized is that thirty-year-old me was probably closer to having his life together than he thought he was.

And forty-two-year-old me owes a lot to the work, the perspective, and even the worries of thirty-year-old me.

This book isn't about having life figured out. It's about what happens when you start asking the right questions and keep moving forward anyway.

This book revisits that list.

Each chapter begins with one of the thirty "absolute truths" I wrote down that weekend. From there, I look back at why I believed it at the time, and how I see it now after another twelve years of life, experience, mistakes, and progress.

The words themselves remain exactly as they were written.

Because that list is a time capsule — a glimpse into the mind of a thirty-year-old man trying to figure things out.

And in a lot of ways, he was doing better than he realized.

The Original List

The following thirty statements are exactly as they appeared in the note I wrote the weekend before my thirtieth birthday. I've left them unchanged.

They reflect the thoughts of a thirty-year-old man trying to make sense of life as it stood at that moment.

Each chapter that follows revisits one of these observations and reflects on how life unfolded over the next twelve years.

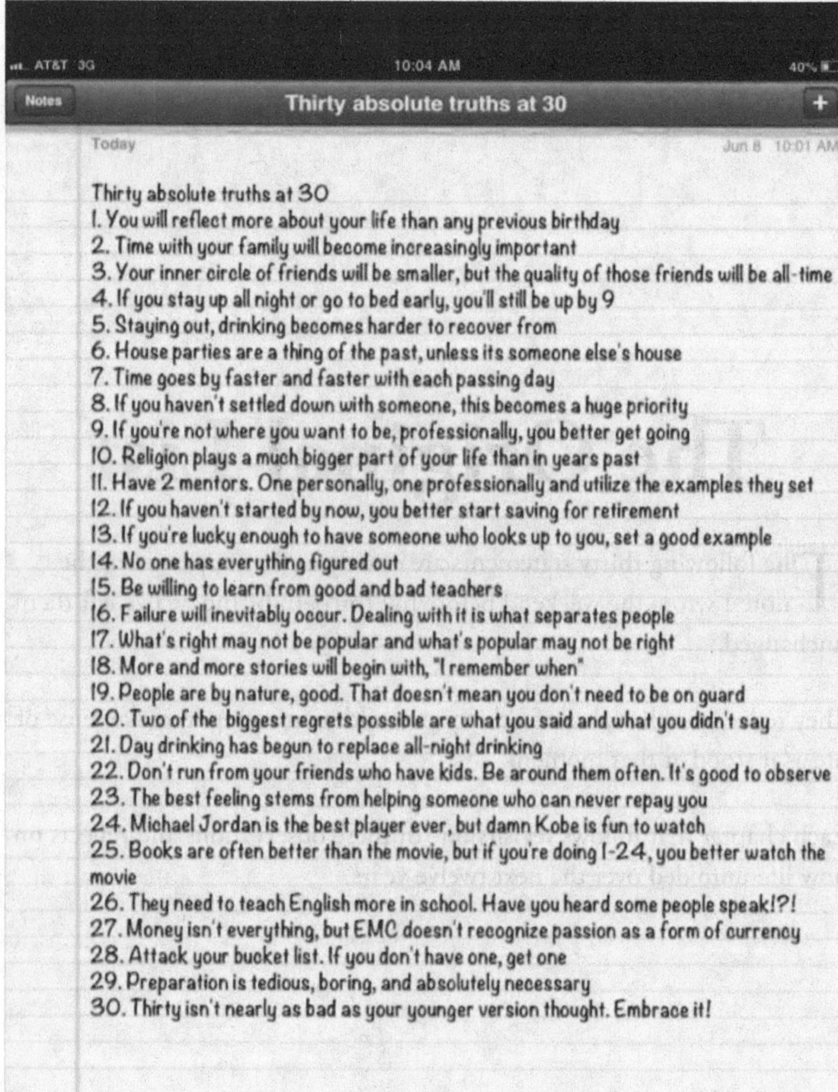

AT&T 3G
10:04 AM
40%
Notes
Thirty absolute truths at 30
+
Today
Jun 8 10:01 AM

Thirty absolute truths at 30
1. You will reflect more about your life than any previous birthday
2. Time with your family will become increasingly important
3. Your inner circle of friends will be smaller, but the quality of those friends will be all-time
4. If you stay up all night or go to bed early, you'll still be up by 9
5. Staying out, drinking becomes harder to recover from
6. House parties are a thing of the past, unless its someone else's house
7. Time goes by faster and faster with each passing day
8. If you haven't settled down with someone, this becomes a huge priority
9. If you're not where you want to be, professionally, you better get going
10. Religion plays a much bigger part of your life than in years past
11. Have 2 mentors. One personally, one professionally and utilize the examples they set
12. If you haven't started by now, you better start saving for retirement
13. If you're lucky enough to have someone who looks up to you, set a good example
14. No one has everything figured out
15. Be willing to learn from good and bad teachers
16. Failure will inevitably occur. Dealing with it is what separates people
17. What's right may not be popular and what's popular may not be right
18. More and more stories will begin with, "I remember when"
19. People are by nature, good. That doesn't mean you don't need to be on guard
20. Two of the biggest regrets possible are what you said and what you didn't say
21. Day drinking has begun to replace all-night drinking
22. Don't run from your friends who have kids. Be around them often. It's good to observe
23. The best feeling stems from helping someone who can never repay you
24. Michael Jordan is the best player ever, but damn Kobe is fun to watch
25. Books are often better than the movie, but if you're doing 1-24, you better watch the movie
26. They need to teach English more in school. Have you heard some people speak!?!
27. Money isn't everything, but EMC doesn't recognize passion as a form of currency
28. Attack your bucket list. If you don't have one, get one
29. Preparation is tedious, boring, and absolutely necessary
30. Thirty isn't nearly as bad as your younger version thought. Embrace it!

Chapter 1

You will reflect more about your life than any previous birthday

My View at 30

When I wrote that line, I was all over the place.

I felt lost. I felt like I didn't have momentum. I was searching, wondering, trying to figure out where I stood in life and whether I was where I should be by that age.

Turning thirty felt like a slap in the face.

It was a wake-up call. A reality check. An urgent call to action.

Up until that point, birthdays had mostly just been birthdays. But thirty felt different. Thirty felt like a line in the sand.

At the time I was in management at a large company. It was a pressure-packed role. The expectations were high and the pace never really slowed down. It was the kind of job where you carried the weight of it with you even after you left the building for the day.

The job itself was demanding, but what made it harder was where I was in life at that moment.

I was away from my family and friends. The people who had always been part of my everyday life were now hours away. That created a sense of loneliness and isolation that I hadn't really experienced before.

Work was stressful, and home didn't necessarily feel like home yet.

It was just where I slept.

I remember evenings sitting in that apartment after work with nothing but quiet around me. No familiar routines, no friends dropping by, no family dinners. Just time to think.

And when life slows down like that, your thoughts get louder.

When you combine pressure at work with isolation outside of work, it leaves you with a lot of time to sit with your own thoughts. And that's exactly what I was doing around that birthday.

Thinking.

Reflecting.

Wondering.

I remember thinking about where I was in life and feeling like I hadn't accomplished enough. Looking back now, I can't even clearly say what I thought I should have accomplished by that age. I just knew I felt behind.

I had never really thought of thirty as old until it suddenly started creeping up on me. A few of my friends were younger than I was and they made sure to remind me of it every chance they got, but even their needling didn't really bother me.

Then for whatever reason, it did. I started thinking about where I was in life and whether I should have been further along by that point.

That's actually what led me to sit down and write the list that became these reflections. As I started putting the thoughts on paper, something else became clear — I still had a lot of runway left and a lot more going for me than I had been giving myself credit for.

The strange part is that I wasn't comparing myself to my closest friends. Many of them were still figuring things out just like I was.

Instead, my mind drifted toward people from high school. People I hadn't spoken to in years but who, from the outside looking in, seemed to have the personal success I thought I was missing.

They seemed settled.

They seemed stable.

They seemed like they had things figured out.

And there I was, sitting in a management job that was grinding on me, living far away from the people I cared about, and feeling like I was stuck in limbo.

It wasn't that there was one specific thing missing.

It was everything.

I wasn't happy at work.

I wasn't happy at home.

I just had this overwhelming sense that there was more out there for me. More opportunity, more fulfillment, more purpose.

The problem was I hadn't figured out how to get there yet.

That uncertainty is what made turning thirty feel so heavy.

It forced me to stop and ask myself questions I had never really asked before.

Where am I going?

Is this the right path?

How long am I going to stay here?

And what am I going to do about it?

For the first time in my life, a birthday didn't just mark another year getting older. It forced me to take inventory of where my life actually stood.

And the more I thought about it, the more I reflected.

My View Now

Looking back, that reflection was real.

I can't speak for everyone else, but for me, turning thirty caused more reflection than any birthday before or since.

It forced me to slow down and take a hard look at my life. At the time it felt uncomfortable, almost like I was standing still while everyone else was moving forward.

But what I didn't realize then is how close I actually was.

Thirty-year-old me thought he was stuck.

He thought he was drifting.

He thought he had fallen behind.

The truth is he was standing right on the edge of a breakthrough.

The very next year I met my wife.

The year after that we were engaged.

Then my career started moving. I received one promotion, then another. The professional momentum that had felt so distant suddenly started showing up.

Before long we bought a house and began building the life that thirty-year-old me had been longing for but couldn't quite see yet.

I was so close.

That's the part that stands out to me now.

At the moment when I felt the most uncertain, when I felt like I hadn't accomplished enough and was somehow behind in life, things were already starting to line up.

I just couldn't see it yet.

Perspective has a way of doing that.

When you're in the middle of a season of uncertainty, it's almost impossible to recognize how close you might be to the next chapter.

All you see is the struggle.

All you feel is the frustration.

All you hear in your head is the voice telling you that you should already be further along.

But sometimes the breakthrough is closer than you think.

If I could sit down with the thirty-year-old version of myself today, the conversation would probably be simple.

First, I would tell him to relax.

Things were going to turn out.

But I would also tell him something important: he was a little out of alignment.

Life tends to move in the right direction when your priorities are aligned with the things that actually matter.

Seek God's approval first. Align your plans with that. Pray regularly. Focus on doing the right things consistently.

When you do that, a lot of the other things you're worried about have a way of taking care of themselves.

Thirty-year-old me didn't have everything figured out.

But he was asking the right questions.

And sometimes asking the right questions is the beginning of everything changing.

I've realized something since then.

The moments when we feel most uncertain about our lives are often the moments right before things begin to change.

Anchor Thought

If you feel behind in life, take a breath. You may be closer than you think.

Chapter 2

Time with your family will become increasingly important

My View at 30

At thirty, I was living about three and a half hours away from my family.

Objectively, that's not very far. It's a long afternoon drive. Something you can do without much planning if you really want to.

But at the time it didn't feel that way.

At the time it felt like three and a half days.

Distance feels different when you're younger and still used to seeing the people you grew up around on a regular basis. When you first move away, even a few hours can feel like you've crossed into a completely different world.

That's where I found myself around thirty.

I had moved away to pursue my career and step into a management role at a large company. The opportunity mattered to me. I wanted to prove something to myself professionally. I wanted to see what I could accomplish if I pushed myself.

But the trade-off was distance.

The people I had grown up with, the people who had always been around — family, friends, familiar places — were no longer part of my everyday life. They were back home.

Three and a half hours away.

And even though that distance doesn't look very large on a map, it felt much bigger when you were living it.

Weeknights were quiet.

Weekends were quieter than I expected.

I had spent most of the previous decade around the same people almost every day, or at the very least every week. Then suddenly that was gone. Instead, I was coming home to a quiet apartment with nothing going on.

I thought a lot about my family and my friends back home and wondered if the sacrifices I was making were really worth it.

For a while I drove home almost every weekend just to be around them again.

My View Now

One evening not long ago, my son asked if we could go outside and throw the football for a few minutes.

I had just finished a long workday and still had work waiting for me, but we went out anyway.

Ten minutes turned into almost an hour.

As we walked back inside, I realized those small moments with family are the ones that end up meaning the most.

Life has a way of expanding your perspective.

Years later my wife and I would move almost twelve hours away from where we started.

That distance really puts things into perspective.

Suddenly three and a half hours doesn't feel very far at all.

Eventually life brought us back closer again, settling within about two and a half hours of home.

But the experiences along the way changed the way I thought about distance, family, and time.

Looking back now, I realize something about the younger version of myself.

He was beginning to understand just how big the world really is.

When you grow up in one place, surrounded by the same people and routines for most of your life, the world can feel small and familiar.

But once you start moving, traveling, and building a life outside of where you started, you begin to see how large it actually is.

And once you see that, you start to appreciate the people who have been part of your life from the beginning even more.

Anchor Thought

The ordinary moments with family are the ones you miss the most later.

Chapter 3

Your inner circle of friends will be smaller, but the quality of those friends will be all-time

My View at 30

By the time I turned thirty, my circle of friends had already started shrinking.

In your early twenties, it feels like you know everyone.

Your social circle is wide.

There are always people around, always something going on, always another group gathering somewhere.

But somewhere along the way that changes.

By thirty, the circle had naturally narrowed.

There were about six to eight of us who were the regulars.

The core group.

Then there were another four to six guys who would join us a few times a month depending on what was going on.

It wasn't intentional.

Nobody sat down and decided who was "in" and who wasn't.

Life just started sorting things out.

The guys who remained were the ones I had the most in common with.

Over time we had gotten to the point where we could practically finish each other's sentences.

We knew each other that well.

Most of us were from the same county and had gone to the same school.

Our ages varied a little, but our lives overlapped in all the ways that mattered.

Some of us were brothers or cousins by blood.

Others were brothers simply because life had bonded us together over time.

My View Now

Twelve years later, the circle is still there.

Life has changed a lot since those days.

We don't spend nearly as many evenings sitting around playing cards or trying to win ridiculous bets.

People have careers now.

Families.

Responsibilities that naturally take priority over hanging out the way we once did.

But the friendships remain.

Today our conversations look a little different.

We still talk sports.

That hasn't changed.

But now we also talk about things we didn't talk about much back then.

Politics.

Careers.

Family.

Faith.

The conversations have grown up a little, just like we have.

Over the years we've seen a lot together.

Promotions.

Rejections.

The highs and the lows that come with building a life.

And those experiences deepen friendships in ways that casual relationships never can.

Anchor Thought

If you're lucky enough to have a few true friends, hold onto them.
They're rarer than you realize.

Chapter 4

If you stay up all night or go to bed early, you'll still be up by 9

My View at 30

In my twenties, staying out late was just part of life.

Most weekends followed a pretty familiar routine. A few of us would start the night at my house, hang out for a while, and then work our way around town. Bars, house parties, wherever the night seemed to take us.

If we were being honest, a big part of the motivation was simple.

We were hoping to meet girls.

That's what a lot of guys in their twenties are doing on weekends.

The nights were long.

We'd stay out way later than I ever would now. Midnight was still early. One or two in the morning wasn't unusual. Sometimes it stretched even later depending on how the night unfolded.

At the time it felt normal.

Sleep wasn't something we thought about very much. You just went out, had fun, stayed up late, and dealt with the consequences the next day.

I can remember a few nights where we were up until the sun came up. The next day was usually pretty brutal. We'd try to sleep it off, but my internal clock rarely allowed that.

Most mornings turned into grabbing some food and hoping for a decent afternoon nap.

Sometimes we'd just head to the golf course and try to sweat it out in the sun while chugging Gatorade.

Even back then it was pretty clear that kind of routine wasn't sustainable.

By the time I was turning thirty, though, my situation had changed a little.

I had moved away for work. During the week I was living about three and a half hours from home. On weekends I would sometimes come back to visit friends and family.

The problem with that arrangement was the timing.

It's one thing to stay out all night when you don't have much to do the next day.

It's another thing entirely when you know you're going to have to wake up and drive three and a half hours back home.

Those mornings were rough.

You'd wake up tired, maybe still feeling the effects of the night before, and then climb into the car for a long drive back.

Caffeine became less of a luxury and more of a necessity.

Even if I stayed out late and tried to sleep in the next morning, I still found myself waking up around the same time.

9 a.m.

It didn't seem to matter if I had stayed out all night or gone to bed early.

My body had found its rhythm whether I liked it or not.

That realization felt like one of those small signals that I wasn't in my early twenties anymore.

I remember one night in my twenties staying out far too late with friends, convinced I could sleep the next morning away.

Sure enough, my eyes popped open early like they always did.

I laid there staring at the ceiling thinking how ridiculous it was that my body had already decided what time the day would start.

My View Now

Looking back, that shift in routine was just part of life moving into a different season.

These days the schedule looks very different.

Most nights we get our son to bed around 8:30.

Once he's down, my wife and I might stay up for a little while longer. Sometimes we watch a game if one's on. Sometimes we scroll on our phones, read something, or just unwind from the day.

But most nights it doesn't take long before we're ready to call it a night.

Around 9:30 the lights go out and the phone goes down.

That routine might sound boring to the twenty-something version of me who used to stay out half the night, but the truth is I appreciate it now.

Part of that change came from work.

My role required early mornings.

My team started early, which meant I needed to start early too.

Over time that became the rhythm of my day.

Eventually I stopped fighting it and started embracing it.

Now I actually enjoy getting up early.

And sleeping until 9 a.m. might happen once a year!

There's something about being awake before the day fully gets moving.

It gives you a head start.

You can think clearly, get organized, and get things done before the rest of the world starts demanding your attention.

More importantly, I've come to appreciate the value of rest.

When you're younger, sleep feels optional.

Something you sacrifice without thinking twice.

But as you get older, you start realizing that good rest affects everything.

Your health.

Your focus.

Your energy.

Even your mood.

These days I rest more than I used to, and my body definitely appreciates it.

If anything, the additional rest is probably adding years onto my life.

And that feels like a pretty good trade.

Anchor Thought

At some point you realize rest isn't boring — it's valuable.

Chapter 5
Staying out, drinking becomes harder to recover from

My View at 30

Before going any further, I should probably acknowledge something up front.

In my twenties, I drank too much and too often.

That's not a confession meant to sound dramatic.

It was simply part of that stage of life.

When you're young and your social life revolves around hanging out with friends, alcohol tends to be part of the environment.

I still enjoy a beer today, but I've learned moderation as I've gotten older, and I'm grateful for that.

Back then, though, drinking was just part of the weekend rhythm.

Most of the time I stuck to beer.

I wasn't someone who mixed a bunch of drinks or chased shots all night.

Because of that, I didn't deal with hangovers very often.

Most of the time.

One time that stands out was a trip to Panama City Beach.

We spent the day on the beach and ended up going out that night with a big group of friends at Spinnakers.

The next day was rough.

The sun and heat made recovering even harder than usual.

I always preferred house parties or sitting outside on a restaurant patio with friends.

A cooler full of beer, a table full of people you enjoy being around, and a long conversation that drifts from sports to life to whatever random topic someone throws out.

That was my favorite version of a night out.

Bars happened occasionally, but I was never a huge fan of them.

I hate cigarettes, and smoke makes me sick.

Back when smoking indoors was still common in a lot of places, walking into a bar sometimes felt like stepping into a cloud of it.

So if I had the choice, I'd take a backyard, a living room, or a patio with friends over a bar any day.

When the night ended and the next morning arrived, the recovery plan was pretty predictable.

You'd sleep as long as you could.

Then you'd go looking for something greasy to eat.

Greasy food always felt like it might somehow soak things up and fix the problem.

And somewhere along the way you'd grab a Gatorade to try to help your body recover.

Most of the time that routine worked well enough.

But by the time I was turning thirty, I had started noticing something.

Recovering from those nights wasn't quite as easy as it had been earlier in my twenties.

Part of that was probably age.

Part of it was the lack of sleep.

And part of it was my internal clock deciding that six in the morning was a perfectly reasonable time to wake up no matter how late the night before had been.

That combination made the mornings a little rougher than they used to be.

My View Now

These days my relationship with drinking looks a lot different.

I still enjoy a beer.

But moderation has become the rule rather than the exception.

Some weekends I might have four to six beers total.

Most weekends I don't have any at all.

One thing that has stayed the same is that I've never been a weekday drinker.

That was true then and it's still true now.

The biggest change isn't really about alcohol itself.

It's about priorities.

Life simply looks different now.

Family.

Work.

Responsibilities that matter more than they used to.

The idea of staying out late just to stay out late doesn't carry the same appeal it once did.

Every now and then my friends and I will joke about turning the clock back and reliving the younger days.

We'll laugh about the stories and the nights we remember.

But once the chuckles fade, the conversation moves on.

No one actually feels the need to go recreate those nights.

And that's probably a sign of maturity more than anything else.

The memories are enough.

The experiences were fun while they lasted.

But life moves forward.

And the older version of me is perfectly content with the balance that exists now.

Anchor Thought

Growing up means learning when enough is enough.

Chapter 6

House parties are a thing of the past, unless it's someone else's house

My View at 30

In my twenties, house parties were a regular part of life.

And more often than not, the house hosting the party was mine.

There were advantages to that arrangement.

The biggest one was simple.

I didn't have to drive anywhere.

Once everyone showed up, I was already where I needed to be.

But there was also a downside.

If things got out of hand, the carnage belonged to me.

Anyone who has hosted enough house parties knows exactly what I'm talking about.

Cups everywhere.

Empty cans scattered around the house.

Furniture moved out of place.

Someone forgetting where they set something down.

And if it happened to be five days before trash pickup and the can was already full, that created a very specific kind of problem.

Those are the details you don't think about when you're younger and planning a night with friends.

The routine for those weekends was pretty predictable.

I'd get off work on Friday afternoon, usually around 3:30 or 4:00.

If I could, I'd try to squeeze in a quick nap before the night got started.

Then the guys would start trickling in sometime between six and eight.

No formal invitations.

No complicated planning.

Everyone just knew where to go.

Once people arrived, the house naturally divided itself into little pockets of activity.

Beer pong outside.

Video games in the living room.

Cards at the dining room table.

The television would usually have whatever big game was on that night.

Neighbors would sometimes wander over.

If someone in the group was dating someone at the time, they might show up with their friends.

Before long there were easily ten or more people hanging out.

Those nights felt effortless.

Nobody needed an itinerary.

Everyone just showed up, found a spot somewhere in the house, and joined whatever conversation or game was happening.

Looking back, it was a really fun season of life.

My View Now

Somewhere along the way, those house parties slowly faded.

There wasn't a specific moment where they stopped.

Life just started changing.

People got busier.

Careers took more time and energy.

Relationships became more serious.

Eventually families started forming.

When that happens, the idea of having ten or fifteen people hanging around your house until late at night doesn't hold the same appeal it once did.

These days when friends get together, it usually looks different.

Maybe it's meeting at a restaurant.

Maybe it's watching a game together.

Maybe it's a cookout where people bring their kids along.

The environment is calmer.

The conversations are different.

And the night usually ends much earlier than it used to.

But the idea of hosting people hasn't completely disappeared.

My wife and I still love having people over for big games, especially Gator game days.

She's a natural and gifted hostess.

And I like to pretend I'm a master chef while working the grill.

Those gatherings look different from the house parties of my twenties, but the spirit behind them is the same.

Good food.

Good friends.

A game on the television.

People enjoying each other's company.

Anchor Thought

Every season of life looks different. Enjoy the one you're in.

Chapter 7

Time goes by faster and faster with each passing day

My View at 30

When I wrote that line, I was starting to notice something that felt strange at the time.

Days seemed normal.

Weeks seemed normal.

But years suddenly felt shorter.

We used to take a trip to Panama City every year for the Fourth of July. After a while it started to feel like we had barely unpacked from the last one before it was time to go again.

In your twenties, time feels wide open. A year feels like a long stretch of life. Five years feels like forever.

By the time I was turning thirty, that feeling had started to change.

Weeks at work would fly by. One Friday would turn into the next before I really stopped to notice it.

You start measuring time differently when you get older.

Instead of thinking about summers or semesters like you did growing up, life starts moving in work weeks, holidays, and calendar years.

And those calendar years begin showing up faster than you expect.

At thirty I was just beginning to notice that shift.

I didn't fully understand it yet, but I could feel it happening.

My View Now

I noticed it one afternoon when I was looking through old photos on my phone. Pictures from what felt like last year were actually three or four years earlier. My son looked smaller in every photo, and the houses we'd lived in blurred together. That's when it really hit me how quickly seasons of life move.

Looking at life from where I stand today, that feeling has only become more real.

When I stop and think about the years since I wrote that list, it almost feels impossible how much has happened.

I've now spent 21 years with the same company.

Since writing that note, I've held six different roles within the organization.

Along the way, life moved too.

I've moved four different times.

I've been married for seven years.

My son is now almost six years old.

That one is probably the clearest reminder of how fast time moves.

One minute you're holding a newborn.

The next minute you're watching him grow into his own little person with opinions, interests, and a personality that makes you laugh every day.

Time moves quickly when you measure it through the growth of your children.

But it also shows up in other ways.

These days I find myself doing things I never would have imagined when I wrote that list at thirty.

I mentor people.

I help guide younger professionals who are trying to figure out their careers.

I think about retirement strategies and what the next decade of work might look like.

I'm exploring side gigs and passive income opportunities that might help create more freedom down the road.

Ten years ago those thoughts weren't even on my radar.

Now they're part of how I think about the future.

When I step back and look at everything that has happened since that note was written, the truth becomes pretty clear.

Time really does move faster with each passing year.

But I've also realized something important.

Time moving faster isn't necessarily a bad thing.

It's just a reminder that life is happening.

Careers develop.

Families grow.

Responsibilities expand.

And before you know it, the person who once felt like he was behind in life is mentoring others who feel the exact same way.

Anchor Thought

One day you look up and realize the years you worried about became the life you hoped for.

Chapter 8

If you haven't settled down with someone, this becomes a huge priority

My View at 30

When I wrote this line, the pressure to settle down wasn't coming from everyone else.

It was coming from me.

There's a point in life where the idea of finding the right person shifts from something you casually think about to something you genuinely start hoping for.

At thirty, I had reached that point.

In my twenties, relationships were part of life but they weren't necessarily the center of it.

You dated.

Sometimes it worked out, sometimes it didn't.

Either way, life kept moving and there was always another distraction waiting around the corner.

Friends.

Work.

Weekend plans.

Travel.

But somewhere around thirty, the perspective starts to change.

You begin noticing the people around you moving into different stages of life.

Friends are getting engaged.

Weddings start appearing on the calendar more often.

Some people are already starting families.

I remember going to a few weddings around that time and realizing something had shifted.

Ten years earlier those receptions felt like big parties.

Now they felt like milestones.

And whether you say it out loud or not, a thought begins to creep in.

Maybe I'd like that too.

It wasn't about some grand vision of the future.

Sometimes it was as simple as finishing a long day and wishing someone was there to talk to about it.

Around that time I even sat down and made a short list of qualities I hoped the woman I married would have.

Nothing complicated.

Just a few things that felt important to me.

She needed to be a non-smoker.

I hoped she would be independent and have a career of her own.

I hoped she would like to travel.

I hoped she would come from a good family.

It wasn't a long list.

But it helped me realize something.

I wasn't just looking for someone to date.

I was looking for someone to build a life with.

My View Now

Looking back, I didn't realize how close that part of my life was to changing.

Within the next year, I met my wife.

The timing of it still feels a little remarkable when I think about it.

The first thing I noticed about her was how engaging she was.

Conversations with her were easy.

She had a way of making people feel comfortable, like she was genuinely interested in what you had to say.

That kind of connection is hard to describe, but you know it when you feel it.

And once we started spending time together, things moved naturally from there.

The following year we were engaged.

Life has a way of moving quickly once the right pieces fall into place.

Now we've been married seven years.

We're raising a son together.

And the life I was hoping to build back then is now the life I get to live every day.

Marriage isn't perfect, and life doesn't suddenly become simple when you find the right person.

But it does make life fuller.

The ordinary moments become more meaningful when you're sharing them with someone who's walking the same path with you.

Looking back now, I can see that the desire I felt at thirty wasn't pressure.

It was readiness.

I was ready for the next stage of life.

I just hadn't met the person yet.

Anchor Thought

If you don't know what you're looking for, you can't find it.

Chapter 9

If you're not where you want to be professionally, you better get going

My View at 30

When I wrote this line, I wasn't unhappy with my job.

In fact, I had a great job.

But there was something about my situation that didn't quite sit right with me.

I was in a leadership role, but it was still fairly close to entry level when you looked at the bigger organizational picture.

That kind of visibility can be a good thing.

But it also means you don't have much room to coast.

At thirty, I was starting to realize something about my career.

There were a lot of opportunities out there.

But opportunities don't usually chase you down.

You have to position yourself to capture them.

Financially, I wasn't exactly where I wanted to be yet.

That realization created a sense of urgency.

I needed to get better.

I needed to push myself harder.

And if I was being completely honest, I needed to start changing the internal perception of who I was and what I was capable of.

My View Now

Looking back now, that sense of urgency turned out to be a good thing.

Instead of drifting professionally, I became more focused.

I started working harder.

I became more vocal about what I wanted to do and how I hoped to get there.

Rather than waiting for opportunities to appear, I began positioning myself for them.

And over time, those opportunities started showing up.

Since writing that list, I've held six different roles within the company.

Each one brought new responsibilities, new challenges, and new opportunities to grow.

Progress doesn't usually happen all at once.

It happens step by step.

A new role.

A new responsibility.

A chance to lead something bigger than you've led before.

Eventually those steps start stacking.

Before you know it, the person who once felt like they needed to "get going" professionally has built a career that includes leadership, mentorship, and experience they never would have imagined earlier.

Anchor Thought

If you want more from your career, be ready when the opportunity shows up.

Chapter 10

Religion plays a much bigger part of your life than in years past

My View at 30

Faith was never something completely absent from my life.

I had always known God.

But knowing God and living closely with Him are not always the same thing.

Around the time I was turning thirty, I could feel that gap in my life.

I believed.

I respected the role faith should play in a person's life.

But if I was being honest with myself, I also knew I wasn't as close to the Lord as I should have been.

At some point in my early thirties, I decided to do something about it.

One year I made a New Year's resolution to read the Bible from beginning to end.

Front to back.

It took discipline and consistency.

But that experience changed something in me.

It gave me perspective I hadn't fully developed before.

My View Now

Looking back, that season was the beginning of a deeper relationship with God.

My faith didn't suddenly change overnight.

It grew year by year.

My wife and I started becoming more involved in church.

Faith became more than something we believed.

It became something we practiced.

Over time that led us to experiences we never would have imagined earlier in life.

We took mission trips to Africa.

We welcomed members of an African worship group into our home.

Those experiences expand your perspective in ways that are hard to fully describe.

Faith has a way of working like that.

Growth doesn't usually happen in one dramatic moment.

It happens gradually.

Year after year.

Looking back now, I can see that the version of me who wrote that list at thirty was aware that faith needed a larger place in my life.

He just didn't fully understand yet how much it would shape the years that followed.

Anchor Thought

Sometimes the most important step of faith is simply planting the seed.

Chapter 11

Have 2 mentors. One personally, one professionally, and utilize the examples they set

My View at 30

I can't claim this was an idea I came up with on my own.

It was something I heard someone say that stuck with me.

I believe it was Glenn Beck who suggested the idea of having two mentors in your life — one to guide you personally and one to guide you professionally.

When I heard that, it immediately made sense.

At thirty, I was beginning to understand that no one succeeds completely on their own.

We all learn from the people around us, whether we realize it or not.

But the more I thought about it, the more I realized something important.

Not every successful person is someone you should model your entire life after.

I had seen examples of this already.

I had known incredibly good people with strong character and great values, but they had no real direction professionally.

At the same time, I had also seen ambitious people climbing the ladder quickly in their careers, but some of their tactics didn't always sit right with me.

Those examples taught me something important.

Success in one area of life doesn't automatically translate into success in another.

That's why the idea of separating mentors into two categories made so much sense.

One mentor to help guide the person you're becoming.

And another to help guide the professional you're becoming.

Each could offer perspective, correction, and inspiration in different ways.

And by learning from both, you could take the best parts of each example while building your own path forward.

My View Now

Looking back, I still believe that advice was incredibly valuable.

Over the years I've been coached hard both personally and professionally.

Some of those conversations were uncomfortable at the time, but they were often the moments that produced the most growth.

One thing I've read over the years is that mentors probably shouldn't be your parents and shouldn't be your direct boss either.

Parents are simply too close to you emotionally.

And bosses are responsible for evaluating your performance.

In both cases it can be difficult to separate those roles from true mentorship.

Some of the best mentoring relationships come from people who have enough distance to speak honestly while still caring about your growth.

I once worked for a leader who had that kind of influence on me.

He was well balanced.

His priorities were straight.

He treated people the right way.

And he was well established professionally.

After our paths eventually went in different directions, he became a mentor to me — whether he knows it or not.

When I'm facing a big career decision or considering a new opportunity, he's one of the people I reach out to.

Personally, I've also learned that wisdom often comes from multiple voices.

When I'm making important life decisions, the first person I turn to is my wife.

After that I often seek perspectives from several people I trust.

My parents.

My mother-in-law.

My brother.

My uncle and aunts.

My old pastor.

Sometimes even close friends.

Each of them sees life from a slightly different perspective.

And when you listen carefully to those perspectives, it helps you see the situation more clearly.

Anchor Thought

Wise people listen to those who have already walked the road.

Chapter 12

If you haven't started by now, you better start saving for retirement

My View at 30

When I wrote this line at thirty, I understood the general idea.

Saving money was important.

Planning for the future was important.

But if I'm being honest, I didn't fully understand how powerful investing could be.

Most of the advice people hear about money is pretty generic.

"Save more."

"Put something away for retirement."

"Make sure you get the company match."

Those are helpful suggestions, but they don't really explain the bigger picture.

Around that time I was also starting to realize something that tied directly into the idea of mentorship from the previous chapter.

Some of the best people you know — great leaders, wonderful parents, loyal friends — may not necessarily be great at investing or managing money.

That doesn't make them any less admirable.

But it does reinforce something important.

Different areas of life require different types of wisdom.

Financial wisdom is one of them.

And if you don't intentionally seek it out, you may never fully understand the opportunities sitting right in front of you.

At thirty, I knew saving mattered.

I just didn't yet appreciate how powerful disciplined investing over time could become.

My View Now

Looking back now, there are several things I wish I had understood earlier.

The biggest one is the power of long-term investing and compounding.

Much later, in my early forties, I read *Rich Dad Poor Dad*, which reinforced many ideas about assets, investing, and financial independence that I had slowly been learning along the way.

The first lesson is simple.

Saving money alone isn't enough.

Your money needs to be working for you.

Another lesson I've learned along the way is this:

Do not allow your debts to grow with your income.

This trap catches a lot of people.

As income increases, lifestyle increases right along with it.

Bigger house.

Bigger car.

Bigger payments.

But when your obligations rise as quickly as your income, financial freedom becomes very difficult to achieve.

Discipline early makes a tremendous difference later.

Anchor Thought

Small financial decisions made consistently over time can completely change your future.

Chapter 13

If you're lucky enough to have someone who looks up to you, set a good example

My View at 30

Even when I wrote this at thirty, I understood that influence carries responsibility.

I'm blessed to have a younger brother, and growing up I always tried to set a good example for him.

Sometimes that meant offering advice.

Other times it meant simply trying to handle things the right way so he could see it.

Over time I had cousins and friends tell me they looked up to me.

Hearing that always made me pause.

When another man tells you he looks up to you, it hits you in a different way.

At thirty, I believed that if someone looked up to you, you had a responsibility to try to live in a way that justified that trust.

Not perfectly.

But honestly.

My View Now

Looking back now, that belief has only grown stronger.

Influence often happens quietly.

People watch how you carry yourself.

How you treat others.

How you respond when things go wrong.

You don't always know when someone is paying attention.

But they are.

And when you realize that someone looks up to you, something changes inside you.

It makes you want to show up better.

Be more thoughtful.

Be more intentional.

Setting a good example isn't about perfection.

It's about consistency.

Doing your best to live with integrity.

Trying to treat people well.

Admitting when you're wrong.

And continuing to work on becoming a better version of yourself.

Anchor Thought

When someone looks up to you, your actions carry more weight than you realize.

Chapter 14
No one has everything figured out

My View at 30

The existence of the thirty truths was proof that I didn't have everything figured out.

If I had life mastered, there would have been no reason to sit down and write a list like that.

At thirty, it felt like you were supposed to have things figured out.

Career direction.

Relationships.

Money.

Life in general.

But I knew I didn't have all the answers.

One phrase that used to bother me was "I don't know."

For a long time those words felt uncomfortable to say.

I thought admitting I didn't know something meant I was less capable.

But the more I looked around at the people in my life, the more I started realizing something important.

Most of us were just trying to figure things out as we went.

And that realization was strangely comforting.

My View Now

Over the years I've met people who seemed to have life perfectly organized from the outside.

Successful careers.

Stable families.

Clear direction.

But the more conversations I had with people like that, the more I realized everyone is still figuring things out in some area of life.

Looking back now, that realization has only grown stronger.

Since turning thirty I've taken on new roles, moved several times, become a husband, and become a father.

Each one of those changes forced me into situations where I didn't automatically have the answers.

And that's okay.

Not knowing something is often the starting point for growth.

Anchor Thought

Growth often begins the moment you're willing to admit you don't have all the answers.

Chapter 15

Be willing to learn from good and bad teachers

My View at 30

When I wrote this at thirty, the idea behind it was simple.

Never stop learning.

There shouldn't be a day that goes by without learning something.

Thankfully, I've been blessed with far more good teachers than bad ones.

But I also started realizing something important.

Learning doesn't only come from great examples.

Sometimes you learn just as much from the examples you don't want to follow.

You can learn what works.

Or you can learn what doesn't.

Both have value.

Professionally, especially, you're constantly observing people around you.

Leadership.

Communication.

How people treat their teams.

How they pursue goals.

Those lessons often come from watching both the good and the bad.

My View Now

Looking back now, that perspective has only grown stronger.

Over the years I've had the opportunity to work under a lot of different leaders.

Most of them taught me something valuable.

Sometimes they showed me exactly how I wanted to lead.

Other times they showed me approaches that didn't sit right with me.

Watching both styles helped me understand something important.

Results matter.

But how you achieve those results matters too.

People deserve to feel valued while pursuing results together.

Sometimes the best lessons don't come from people who show you exactly what to do.

Sometimes they come from people who show you what you don't want to become.

Anchor Thought

Every teacher offers a lesson — even the ones you shouldn't follow.

Chapter 16

Failure will inevitably occur. Dealing with it is what separates people

My View at 30

At the time I wrote this list, I was convinced I was more of a failure than anything.

Of course, that's being a bit dramatic and throwing quite the pity party, but that's honestly how it felt in that moment. I was looking at where I thought I should be in life and comparing it to where I actually was, and it didn't feel like I measured up.

What I didn't fully appreciate then was that failure isn't always what it appears to be.

In my twenties I had been told no when I pursued a leadership position at work. At the time that rejection felt like a failure. It felt like confirmation that I wasn't where I needed to be.

But about a year later, I earned that same opportunity.

Looking back now, was that really a failure? Or was it simply a lesson in what it would take to succeed?

The same thing applied to relationships.

I had dated women who ultimately weren't right for me. At the time those relationships ending felt like failures too. But eventually I met the woman who would become my wife.

Those earlier experiences forced me to recalibrate what I was looking for and what truly mattered.

Even friendships followed that pattern.

There were friendships I lost along the way because, for one reason or another, I hadn't upheld my end of the bargain. At the time those situations felt like failures as well.

But they also forced me to reflect on how I could be a better friend.

Looking back now, I realize something important.

What I was calling failure was often just a lesson I hadn't recognized yet.

My View Now

Years later, I can say with confidence that I was wrong about one thing.

I wasn't a failure.

I never was.

But I have failed plenty of times.

And I still do occasionally.

Failure is inevitable. Anyone who tries to accomplish anything meaningful in life will eventually run into it.

The real separation between people isn't whether failure occurs.

It's how they deal with it.

Some people allow failure to define them.

Others study it, learn from it, and move forward better prepared than before.

Looking back now, the most interesting part is realizing that even during that period when I felt like I was failing, I already understood this truth.

I had written it down.

I had the answer then, even in the middle of my pity party.

I just wasn't applying it yet.

Anchor Thought

Failure is inevitable. Growth comes from how you respond to it.

Chapter 17

What's right may not be popular and what's popular may not be right

My View at 30

When I wrote this at thirty, it wasn't a new idea.

Variations of it have existed for a long time.

But it was something I had started to recognize more clearly in my own life.

You can't base decisions — especially as a leader — on what's popular.

Popularity can be loud.

When enough people lean one direction, it can start to feel like that must be the right direction simply because it's supported by the crowd.

But leadership requires something different.

It requires stepping back, thinking through a situation carefully, deciding the course of action you believe is right, and then standing firm in that decision.

Even when it isn't popular.

At thirty I was beginning to understand that doing the right thing doesn't always come with applause.

Sometimes it means disappointing people.

Sometimes it means walking away from something that others would happily continue.

Those moments force you to decide what matters more — approval or integrity.

My View Now

Looking back now, that truth has only become clearer.

Leadership can be lonely.

The decisions that are right aren't always the ones that make people happy. They don't always win popularity contests.

Sometimes the right decision hurts.

Sometimes you're choosing the best option out of a group of bad options.

I've experienced that firsthand.

At work there have been times when I had to part ways with team members who were well liked by others.

They weren't bad people and their mistakes weren't intentional or egregious, but policies had been violated.

Those moments are difficult.

You know the decision won't be popular, but ignoring it would be worse.

Moments like those reinforce something important.

When you're responsible for others — or even just responsible for yourself — you can't make decisions based on what earns the most approval in the moment.

You have to think about what's right for the long term.

Popularity fades quickly.

But the consequences of decisions tend to last much longer.

Anchor Thought

The right decision won't always be popular, but you'll be able to live with it.

Chapter 18

More and more stories will begin with, "I remember when"

My View at 30

When I wrote this at thirty, I had started noticing something in conversations.

More and more stories seemed to begin the same way.

"I remember when…"

Maybe it's because earlier in life there simply isn't enough experience yet to have many of those stories.

But even then, I had started seeing glimpses of it.

When my friends and I would get together, we would already find ourselves reminiscing about things we had done together.

Nights out.

Trips we took.

Ridiculous bets.

Games we watched.

Things that happened that only our group would understand.

We would laugh and say things like, "Remember when…"

Those were the days when we felt ten feet tall and bulletproof.

Even at thirty I could tell those stories were only going to grow with time.

My View Now

Looking back now, that observation has proven completely true.

As I've gotten older, I've realized I've lived an interesting life — at least according to some people.

I've had a long career that has taken me to different places.

I've moved several times, taken on new roles, and faced new challenges.

Along the way I got married, became a father, and walked through some of life's harder moments as well.

Life has a way of giving you stories whether you're looking for them or not.

And I've noticed something about those conversations.

A lot of my answers now start the same way.

"I remember when…"

Those stories aren't just nostalgia.

They're perspective.

They're lessons.

They're reminders of where you've been and how far you've come.

Anchor Thought

Stories that begin with "I remember when" are often lessons in disguise.

Chapter 19

People are by nature, good. That doesn't mean you don't need to be on guard

My View at 30

By the time I wrote this list at thirty, I felt like I had lived enough life to understand something about people.

Not everyone is out to get you.

But not everyone has your best interests in mind either.

I've always tried to be more of a glass-half-full kind of person.

I tend to believe most people are good.

I think more people want to see others do well than want to see them fail.

At the same time, it only takes a few bad apples to remind you that you still need to pay attention.

There are people who try to sow discord for reasons that aren't always clear.

Sometimes it's jealousy.

Sometimes insecurity.

At thirty I was beginning to understand that both of those things could be true at the same time.

Most people are good.

But wisdom requires you to stay aware.

My View Now

Looking back now, that belief hasn't changed.

If anything, it has grown stronger.

I've seen too many examples of people stepping up for others to believe that most people are bad.

At the same time, experience has taught me that you can't move through life completely unaware.

The good people in your life will build you up.

Others may try to tear things down for reasons that have more to do with them than with you.

So the balance becomes simple.

Trust people until they give you a reason not to.

Believe they're good until they prove otherwise.

Starting with trust is still the better way to live.

Anchor Thought

Most people are good. Wisdom teaches you when to trust and when to be careful.

Chapter 20

Two of the biggest regrets possible are what you said and what you didn't say

My View at 30

When I wrote this line at thirty, I was beginning to notice something about relationships.

Words carry weight.

The things we say can build people up or tear them down in an instant.

But I was also starting to realize that silence can carry weight too.

At that stage of life, I probably wasn't as willing to express my emotions as I should have been.

A lot of people are like that when they're younger.

You assume people know how you feel.

You assume there will always be time to say the things you're thinking.

But the truth is, sometimes we hold things back.

We don't say thank you.

We don't tell someone we appreciate them.

We don't say we're proud of someone.

And we don't always apologize when we should.

At the same time, the opposite problem can happen too.

You can say something in anger or frustration that you immediately wish you could take back.

Both types of moments can leave lasting regret.

My View Now

Looking back now, that realization has only become clearer.

Life has brought moments that make you reflect more deeply.

Losing family members and friends reminds you that time is not unlimited.

Situations like that make you realize how important it is to express love, gratitude, and appreciation while you still have the opportunity.

At the same time, growing older also brings a different kind of awareness.

When I think back to some things I said in my earlier years — joking with friends or reacting in frustration — I realize there were moments when I should have practiced more restraint.

Words spoken casually can still carry weight.

That's why learning to guard your words matters in both directions.

Be careful with words spoken in anger.

But also be willing to speak the words that strengthen the people around you.

Anchor Thought

Guard your words. Avoid the ones spoken in anger, and don't withhold the ones someone needs to hear.

Chapter 21

Day drinking has begun to replace all-night drinking

My View at 30

By the time I wrote this list at thirty, I had done more all-night drinking and more day drinking than I should have.

Those years were part of life at that stage. Friends getting together, staying out late, chasing the night a little longer than we should have. At the time it just felt normal.

Looking back, I have more foggy nights than I'm proud to admit.

But those years weren't a total waste either. Some of my lifelong friendships were built during those days, and there are plenty of good memories mixed in with the blurry ones.

In my twenties we got together every Saturday and watched college football.

We watched the noon games, the 3:30 window, and the night games.

Some weekends we'd have thirty or more people packed into the house watching games on multiple TVs.

The same core group I mentioned earlier was there almost every weekend. Other friends would flow in and out depending on schedules and which games people wanted to watch.

It was a blast.

Around that time I also started noticing a shift.

Instead of staying out all night, it became more common to meet up during the day.

Watching a game.

Cooking out.

Having a few beers in the afternoon instead of pushing everything into the middle of the night.

It wasn't a complete change overnight, but the shift had started.

My View Now

Looking back now, the biggest lesson from those years is moderation.

I eventually learned it, but I'd encourage people to master it sooner rather than later.

Your mind, your body, and the people in your vicinity will thank you.

Shifting things earlier in the day does make a difference too.

You sleep better.

You recover better.

Your body appreciates the change.

What hasn't changed is how much I enjoy getting together with family and friends.

We don't gather for full Saturdays of football like we used to, but we still find ways to get together.

Now we'll plan trips around a big game and spend the weekend together.

Sometimes we'll travel to watch the Florida Gators play football or basketball.

It's always a blast.

The difference now is we're more mindful of when the game starts and when it ends.

We pace ourselves and try not to overdo it.

Watching a good game, cooking out, and having a beer with friends is still something I enjoy today.

The difference now is that it happens with moderation.

Anchor Thought

Good friends and good times are worth keeping. Learning moderation makes them even better.

Chapter 22

Don't run from your friends who have kids. Be around them often. It's good to observe

My View at 30

When I wrote this at thirty, I didn't have kids of my own.

I didn't even have nieces or nephews at the time.

My experience around children was minimal, and for a long time I wasn't even sure I wanted kids.

As thirty approached, though, that stance started to soften.

I began realizing that I wanted a legacy, and the most natural way that happens is through family.

At the same time, I also understood that if I was going to have kids one day, the most important decision I would ever make would be choosing who their mother would be.

That mattered more than anything else.

Around that time some of my friends had started having kids.

When I was back in town, I would spend time around them and their families.

I can remember being at a friend's house where we'd play cards or watch football.

He and his wife had a three-year-old at the time.

Up until then I had mostly thought of kids as interruptions to the kinds of things we were used to doing.

But being around them started to change that perception.

Kids began to seem less like interruptions and more like additions.

Even though I wasn't a parent yet, observing those moments started to shift my thinking.

My View Now

Looking back now, I completely endorse this truth.

Being around your friends who have kids is a great experience, even if you don't have children of your own yet.

You learn by watching.

You see how parents interact with their kids.

You see the patience it requires.

The responsibility it brings.

And the joy that comes along with it.

It also broadens your world.

Spending time around friends and their kids introduces you to new people, new conversations, and new experiences you might not otherwise have.

What starts as simply spending time with friends often becomes an opportunity to learn something about family and responsibility.

Anchor Thought

Sometimes the best preparation for your future is observing the lives around you today.

Chapter 23

The best feeling stems from helping someone who can never repay you

My View at 30

Even when I wrote this line at thirty, I already believed strongly in the idea of helping others.

Charity always made sense to me.

But I also believed there was an important distinction in how that help should be offered.

I've always felt there's a difference between extending a hand up and extending a hand out.

A hand up helps someone get back on their feet.

A hand out can sometimes create dependency.

Over time you realize there are people who genuinely need help and appreciate it, and there are also people who will take advantage of generosity if given the opportunity.

Finding that balance is important.

The goal isn't to rescue people from every problem they face.

The goal is to help people who are trying to move forward but just need a little support along the way.

My View Now

Looking back now, I've had several opportunities in life to see how meaningful that kind of help can be.

There have been seasons when people close to me were struggling to find direction in life.

Friends who needed a place to land while they figured things out.

At different times I was fortunate enough to help them.

Sometimes that meant letting a friend crash on my couch for a while.

I didn't expect anything in return.

I simply believed that if you're able to help someone who needs it, you should.

Years later it's been incredibly rewarding to see how those same friends' lives have unfolded.

Many of them now have careers.

They own homes.

They have families of their own.

Watching someone find their footing after a difficult season is one of the most satisfying things you can witness.

Anchor Thought

The greatest kind of generosity expects nothing in return.

Chapter 24

Michael Jordan is the best player ever, but d*** Kobe is fun to watch

My View at 30

I've been a huge sports fan my entire life, and I've loved basketball since I was a kid.

I remember staying up late to watch games and sneaking my TV back on during school nights after my parents had already told me to turn it off.

If there was a big game on, I wanted to see it.

I even had a goal mounted on my bedroom door growing up.

My brother and I would spend hours battling each other and holding dunk contests in the house.

Around the time I was coming into my teens, Michael Jordan was starting his second three-peat with the Chicago Bulls.

I saw his greatness firsthand and heard the pundits constantly talk about him being the greatest player of all time.

It was hard to argue.

During that same period, Kobe Bryant came into the league.

We weren't that far apart in age, and I immediately loved his confidence.

He had charisma.

He had swagger before we even called it that.

My View Now

Looking back now, I still see it the same way.

Michael Jordan is the greatest player ever.

But Kobe Bryant was incredible to watch.

Kobe went on some unbelievable scoring runs.

An 81-point game.

Nine straight forty-point games.

Four straight fifty-point games.

All during an era when the NBA still prided itself on defense.

But what stood out most wasn't just his talent.

It was how relentlessly he worked to improve.

And how fiercely he competed every single night.

Now I find myself telling my son stories about Kobe.

About his work ethic.

His resilience.

His mental toughness.

Those are the traits I hope my son sees when he hears those stories.

Anchor Thought

Greatness earns respect, but relentless work and resilience are what truly inspire people.

Chapter 25

Books are often better than the movie, but if you're doing 1–24, you better watch the movie

My View at 30

To be honest, this one was mostly an attempt at humor.

If you were busy doing the first twenty-four things on this list, there probably wasn't a lot of time left to sit down and read a thousand-page book like *The Lord of the Rings*.

In that case, you might as well just watch the movie and save yourself some time.

The truth behind the joke, though, was that books are usually better than the movies made from them.

Books give you more detail.

More context.

More depth.

They allow the story to unfold in ways a two-hour film simply can't.

My View Now

As I've gotten older, that basic idea hasn't really changed.

Books are still almost always better than the movie.

Reading forces you to slow down and think.

It stretches your imagination and exposes you to new ideas and perspectives.

Movies are still great entertainment, but they're usually the shortcut version of a much deeper story.

That said, the humor in the original thought still holds true.

Life can be busy.

If you're actually doing the work required to grow personally and professionally, your time becomes more limited.

In those moments, sometimes watching the movie is just the practical option.

Anchor Thought

Books usually tell the better story, but sometimes life moves fast and the movie will do.

Chapter 26

They need to teach English more in school. Have you heard some people speak?!

My View at 30

When I wrote this one at thirty, it was mostly meant to be tongue in cheek.

There was definitely humor behind it. Everyone has heard someone speak in a way that makes you stop and wonder if they ever paid attention in English class.

But underneath the joke there was some seriousness too.

Even then, it felt like proper English, grammar, and spelling were starting to slip.

It seemed like fewer people cared about speaking clearly or writing correctly.

Communication is such a basic skill, yet it often felt like it was being treated as unimportant.

The line itself was written for a laugh, but the observation behind it was real.

My View Now

Looking back now, I actually think the problem has gotten worse.

Today everything has autocorrect.

There are squiggly lines under words that fix spelling mistakes for us.

Phones and computers correct our writing automatically before we even notice the error.

The tools have become smarter than the way many people use them.

The bigger issue is that things we had to learn when I was younger are now being outsourced to devices and artificial intelligence.

When the tools do the work for you, the learning never fully takes place.

That creates a gap that can last a lifetime if it isn't closed.

Clear communication still matters.

Being able to speak well, write clearly, and express ideas properly is an incredibly valuable skill in every part of life — personally, professionally, and academically.

What started as a humorous observation has become more of a warning.

Technology can help us communicate more efficiently, but it shouldn't replace the effort required to learn how to think, write, and speak clearly in the first place.

Anchor Thought

Technology should assist communication, not replace the responsibility of learning how to communicate well.

Chapter 27

Money isn't everything, but EMC doesn't recognize passion as a form of currency

My View at 30

When I wrote this one, I was thinking about the reality of the working world.

Passion is important. People should absolutely pursue things they enjoy and feel called toward.

But I was beginning to realize that the marketplace doesn't always reward passion alone.

At the time, I was seeing more and more stories about people earning degrees that didn't necessarily translate into strong job opportunities.

They had followed something they loved, but when it came time to enter the workforce, the options were limited.

Passion didn't always pay the bills.

It wasn't meant to discourage people from pursuing their interests.

It was more of a recognition that the world runs on economics whether we like it or not.

Companies compensate people based on the value they create, not simply how passionate they are about the work.

My View Now

Early in my career I watched a few people who approached their work with genuine enthusiasm.

They weren't always the most experienced or the most technically skilled, but their energy stood out.

Over time I saw how that passion opened doors for them that talent alone sometimes didn't.

As I've gotten older, I still largely agree with the spirit of that observation.

Passion is a wonderful thing and everyone should try to find it somewhere in their life.

But passion alone doesn't keep the lights on.

Dollars do.

Most of us work to support our lives, our families, and our future.

Ideally we find work that we enjoy and feel proud of.

But financial stability still matters.

Earning, saving, and investing wisely are what eventually give people the freedom to choose how they spend their time later in life.

Anchor Thought

Passion can guide your choices, but financial discipline is what ultimately creates freedom.

Chapter 28

Attack your bucket list. If you don't have one, get one

My View at 30

The movie *The Bucket List* had been out a few years when I wrote this, and it got my wheels turning.

The idea of intentionally setting goals for fun experiences really resonated with me.

We regularly set goals for things like health or wealth, but not nearly as often for the things we simply want to experience in life.

Life can easily become a routine of work, responsibilities, and obligations.

Having things you genuinely look forward to doing — places to go, experiences to have, memories to make — felt like an important reminder that life isn't only about the grind.

My View Now

That idea still holds true today.

Health goals matter.

Wealth goals matter.

But fun goals matter too.

We work hard in life, and part of the reason we work hard is so we can enjoy the experiences that make life memorable.

I've traveled to roughly half the states in America.

I've been to three continents and around a dozen countries.

I've seen Kobe Bryant and Tom Brady play live.

I've attended a PGA Championship.

I've been to incredible bowl games and huge games at Ben Hill Griffin Stadium — better known as The Swamp.

Many of those adventures have been with family and friends.

Much of my broader travel has been with my wife.

Now I'm excited to share that same love of travel and adventure with our kids.

Anchor Thought

Work helps build a life, but experiences are what make that life memorable.

Chapter 29
Preparation is tedious, boring, and absolutely necessary

My View at 30

Preparation largely isn't fun.

Getting ready for a tour of your route or area comes with a lot of preparation.

You have to know the details, anticipate questions, and make sure everything is in order before anyone arrives.

None of that work is glamorous.

In fact, most of it is tedious.

But when the preparation pays off and everything goes well, the payoff is awesome.

The confidence that comes from being ready makes the moment worthwhile.

Even then I understood that the results people see are often built on hours of quiet preparation that nobody else notices.

My View Now

That lesson has only become more true over time.

I've had many moments in my career where preparation made the difference between success and embarrassment.

Today my preparation looks a little different.

Much of it revolves around being ready to present facts and information clearly.

Professionally or personally, you never want to get caught unprepared.

Doing the work ahead of time may not feel exciting, but it protects you from avoidable mistakes.

I've always admired Kobe Bryant's mindset when he talked about confidence coming from preparation.

If I've prepared, I'm rarely nervous when I present.

Preparation builds confidence.

Anchor Thought

Preparation may be tedious, but it turns nervous moments into confident ones.

Chapter 30
Thirty isn't nearly as bad as your younger version thought. Embrace it!

My View at 30

When I was younger, turning thirty felt like a much bigger deal than it actually turned out to be.

Somewhere along the way, thirty had been built up in my mind as this major threshold.

A line you crossed where life was supposed to suddenly change.

Thirty felt like the age where you were supposed to have everything figured out.

Career in place.

Family started.

Life direction clear.

And if you hadn't accomplished those things yet, it was easy to feel like you were behind.

That feeling was part of what led me to write the original list.

But when the day actually arrived, something interesting happened.

My hair didn't fall out.

It didn't turn gray overnight.

And no one came by to move me into a nursing home.

Instead of feeling like the beginning of the end, it felt more like a moment of perspective.

My View Now

Looking back now, turning thirty was actually one of the most important turning points in my life.

Writing that list forced me to pause and evaluate where I was and where I wanted to go.

Instead of feeling like I had run out of time, it felt like I had reached a point where I could start making more intentional decisions.

Turning thirty didn't welcome me into the final stages of life.

It welcomed me into the stage where life started making more sense.

In the years that followed, many of the things I hoped for began to unfold.

I met my wife.

My career grew.

My perspective matured.

Turning thirty wasn't the beginning of the end.

It was the beginning of some of the best years of my life.

Anchor Thought

Turning thirty isn't the closing chapter of youth. For many people, it's the beginning of their most meaningful years.

Closing Thoughts

Looking back now, thirty-year-old me got a lot of things right.

But he also got a few things wrong.

He thought life should already be figured out.

He thought everyone else was further ahead.

He thought success meant reaching certain milestones by certain ages.

What he didn't understand yet was that life rarely moves according to a schedule.

Sometimes the things you're waiting for are already on their way.

You just can't see them yet.

Every now and then I still pull up that note on my phone.

The same list I wrote the weekend before I turned thirty.

Thirty truths that felt important at the time.

Some of them turned out exactly right.

Some of them changed as life unfolded.

But the most important thing about that list wasn't the answers.

It was the questions.

Because asking those questions was the beginning of the life I was hoping to build.

Looking back now, the questions I was asking that weekend weren't signs that I was lost.

They were signs that I was starting to pay attention.

And sometimes that's the real turning point.

Not when everything suddenly becomes clear.

But when you begin to think more carefully about the life you want to live.

If I could give one piece of advice to someone standing where I was that weekend, it would be this:

Accept that you are not nearly as in control as you might think you are — and that's actually a good thing.

Life is less about imposing your will on the world and more about how you respond to what unfolds in front of you.

Align your plans with God.

Listen carefully for His direction.

And be willing to act when the path becomes clear.

Because when the time comes, things can move faster than you expect.

Thirty-year-old me thought he was trying to figure life out.

What he was really doing was beginning the work of building it.

About the Author

Kevin Horton is a husband, father, and business leader who has spent more than two decades building a career in management while raising a family and deepening his faith.

Over the years he has moved across several states, held multiple leadership roles, and mentored young professionals navigating the early stages of their careers. His work has taken him through different seasons of life that have shaped his perspective on leadership, responsibility, faith, and the importance of building a meaningful life.

Kevin writes about lessons learned through experience — faith, family, work, friendship, and the small moments that shape a life. His writing reflects a belief that growth comes from reflection, discipline, and a willingness to keep learning through every stage of life.

He lives with his wife and son, with another child on the way, and continues pursuing a life built on intentionality, gratitude, and service.

Other Books by Kevin Horton

Stewarded Influence

Faithful Leadership in a Performance-Driven World

A practical look at leadership, responsibility, and the influence we carry in the workplace and beyond. This book explores how faith, character, and intentional leadership shape the people and organizations we serve.

Raising Builders

A Father's Letters to His Sons on Faith, Discipline, and the Men God Intended Them to Become

A collection of letters written from a father to his sons about character, faith, responsibility, and the kind of men worth becoming.

Financial Lessons I Wish I Knew

Avoid Costly Money Mistakes, Build Real Assets, and Achieve Financial Freedom

A reflection on financial mistakes, lessons learned, and the practical habits that help people build wealth, invest wisely, and move toward financial independence.

Built to Last

What I've Learned, What I'm Learning, and What I Don't Know Yet About Marriage

A practical reflection on the lessons learned through marriage — communication, commitment, faith, and the daily choices that build a strong and lasting relationship.